DISCARD

Inventions That Shaped the World

THE CAMERA

TRUDI STRAIN TRUEIT

Franklin Watts
A Division of Scholastic Inc.
New York • Toronto • London • Auckland • Sydney
Mexico City • New Delhi • Hong Kong
Danbury, Connecticut

For William, whose photographs touch my soul

Photographs © 2006: Art Resource, NY: 24 (Bridgeman-Giraudon), 16 (HIP), 49 (Réunion des Musées Nationaux), 42, 47 (Victoria & Albert Museum, London); Bridgeman Art Library International Ltd., London/New York: 13 (Deir el-Medina, Thebes, Egypt), 40 (National Museum of Photography, Film & Television); Classic PIO Partners: cover left, chapter opener-antique camera; Corbis Images: 26, 61 (Bettmann), 7 (Kevin P. Casey), 64 (Jon Feingersh); Getty Images/Hulton Archive: 41 (Spencer Arnold), 45 (Eadweard Muybridge), 19; Library of Congress: cover bottom right, 30, 43 52; Mary Evans Picture Library: 51; Peter Arnold Inc./ Alfred Pasieka: 37; Photo Researchers, NY/Mehau Kulyk: 65; Superstock, Inc.: cover top right, chapter opener-contemporary camera (Nicholas Eveleigh), 10 (Explorer); The Art Archive/ Picture Desk: 20 (Marc Charmet), 55 (National Archives, Washington D.C.), 54 (Laurie Platt Winfrey); The Image Works: 66 (Amanda Morris), 35, 59, 63 (NMPFT/SSPL), 23 (SSPL), 62 (Topham).

Illustration by J. T. Morrow

Cover design by The Design Lab
Book production by The Design Lab

Library of Congress Cataloging-in-Publication Data
Trueit, Trudi Strain.
  The camera / Trudi Strain Trueit.
       p. cm. — (Inventions that shaped the world)
  Includes bibliographical references and index.
  ISBN 0-531-12409-6 (lib.bdg.)   0-531-13900-X (pbk.)
  1. Cameras—History—Juvenile literature. I. Title. II. Series.
  TR250.T77 2006
  771.3—dc22   2005026271

CONTENTS

CHAPTER ONE

A TOUCH OF MAGIC

"Smile!"

Grinning broadly, you strike a pose and wait for the flash. "Perfect," says your best friend, hurrying toward you. Before you can blink the spots out of your eyes, there it is: your image grinning at you from a small screen on a *digital camera.* A split second of your life has been captured forever. Or, at least, until you notice the red licorice stuck in your teeth. No problem. With the push of a button, the photo is erased and you're ready to try again.

Today, commercial cameras are so affordable, portable, and easy to use that it is no wonder there are more than 200 million of them in the United States. That's one for nearly every adult in the nation. People rely on cameras for many things: recording memories, documenting events, communication, identification, and expressing themselves.

Photography has become such an important part of the culture that most people can hardly imagine life without it. Yet fewer than two hundred years ago, the camera did not even exist. To those who witnessed the birth of photography in the middle of the nineteenth century, seeing an image of reality appear on a metal plate must have seemed like magic. In a way, it was.

Photo Fanatics

The invention of the camera gave people the power to seize a moment in time, hold it in their hands, and share it with others. Photography was intriguing. It was mysterious. It was a bit scary. But from the start, humanity was fascinated. In the early days of photography, people would stand in long lines for hours simply to have their *portraits* taken. Rapid improvements in camera design gave individuals the ability to get behind the lens to record everyday life for themselves. And eagerly, they did just that.

Over time, cameras went beyond preserving the past to playing a key role in the present. In the twenty-first century, cameras are all around us. Worldwide, it is estimated that about 25 million security cameras keep an eye on everyone from window shoppers to drivers who run red lights. In space, cameras attached to satellites allow some scientists to track changing weather patterns, while others learn more about distant stars and planets. Capsule cameras, so named because they're about the size of a cold capsule, are swallowed by patients so doctors can search inside the human body for disease. Many forms of modern communication depend on cameras to educate, inform,

Video cameras are used to monitor security in airports and many other locations.

advertise, and entertain. From trading cards to textbooks, cereal boxes to billboards, the average American views about one thousand photos every day.

Photographs, in turn, have a magic all their own. They are a mirror of the world—past, present, and future. From the intricate detail of a butterfly's wing to the horrors of war, pictures reflect all that is beautiful and ugly, good and evil, right and wrong. They evoke powerful emotions, influence opinions, and spark controversy. At times, these images even prompt humanity to take action. "The camera is an instrument that teaches people how to see without a camera," explained photographer Dorothea Lange (1895–1965). Her revealing images of human suffering in the Dust Bowl region of the United States during the Great Depression touched the heart of the nation.

In the few minutes it has taken you to read this introduction, nearly 500,000 new photos have been snapped around the globe—roughly 2,700 images per second! Why are we pressing the shutter at such a dizzying rate? Maybe it is because in a world where things change so quickly, we long to freeze time to look at life more closely. Perhaps it is human nature for us to want to chronicle our existence so that others will remember us. Or it might be our way of holding on to the here and now: taking one lazy summer afternoon with your best friend and inviting it to stay forever.

CHAPTER TWO

IMITATING LIFE

Long before the invention of the camera, people were copying reality with a keen eye and a skilled hand. More than 50,000 years ago, early humans scratched pictures onto the bones of animals using crude tools made of flint. By 35,000 B.C., Stone Age artists were carving small human and animal figurines from ivory, antlers, and stones. They also began to paint scenes on rock using pigments, or colors, found naturally in plants and soil. Some of the pigments they used were red *ochre,* yellow ochre, and charcoal.

Prehistoric artists in Europe, Australia, Africa, and the Middle East painted images on slabs of stone. Wind and weather destroyed much of their exposed work. But many examples of *Paleolithic* cave art have survived underground. One of the most spectacular sites is the Chauvet-

Prehistoric artists created this rock painting of hunters with animals at Sefar, Algeria.

Pont-D'Arc in southeastern France. Discovered by French explorers in 1994, the cavern is a wonderland of paintings, drawings, and engravings dating back 32,000 years. They are the oldest known cave paintings.

Most of the three hundred images are of animals, including rhinoceroses, lions, horses, bears, and mammoths. Stamps and stencils of human hands are also visible. Stamps were created by coating the palm with red ochre before pressing the palm against a rock face. Stencils were made by placing one hand against a wall and blowing pigment over it. Scientists believe that the artists at Chauvet not only sought to portray their world accurately, but also may have wanted to leave images of themselves behind.

Staying Inside the Lines

In 5,000 B.C., artists in Egypt painted the tomb walls of their pharaohs with scenes from daily life, such as farming and fishing. These images were meant to ensure the pharaohs held positions of power in the afterlife.

Artists, who were viewed as unskilled laborers, showed a pharaoh as he longed to be—not as he truly was. In a painting, the pharaoh was portrayed as taller than everyone else. Carved from granite or slate, a pharaoh's statue was stiff and angular. This did not change until Akhenaton, who ruled from 1353 to 1335 B.C., established a religion around the sun god. This new emphasis on nature gave Egyptian artists and sculptors permission to use curved lines and proper scale to create more realistic images.

Coloring the World

The Egyptians made some of the earliest tempera paints. Artists ground pigments into powder and mixed them with other ingredients to help the paint bind, or stick, to a surface. These binding agents included animal fat, fish glue, plant juices, blood, and egg whites. Nearly seven thousand years later, eggs whites would come in handy again, this time to help print early photographs on glass, metal, and paper.

Dating from the 900s B.C., sculptors in Greece crafted statues of historical figures, warriors, and athletes in stone, bronze, and terra cotta (baked clay). Early figures were formal and geometric. But by the sixth century B.C., sculptors were allowed to more closely follow the human form. They included physical details, such as hair and clothing. In the mid-fifth century B.C., a painter named Polygnotus broke new ground by giving his subjects facial expressions. He positioned people so they appeared closer or farther away from the edge of the painting. Other painters, such as Apollodorus, Zeuxis, and Apelles also sought to bring realism and emotion to their work. None of their creations survived to modern times, but descriptions of them did.

During the era of the Roman Empire (27 B.C.–A.D. 476), sculptors excelled in capturing the character of their subjects in marble and bronze. It was common for statues of the current emperor to be displayed in public buildings. The images were meant to glorify the ruler who, of course, had to approve of his likeness. Scenes from daily life, myths, and historical battles were also important themes in Roman mosaics, murals, and wooden panel paintings.

Today, few Greek and Roman paintings remain. In the late nineteenth century, however, archaeologists discovered the first of the Fayum mummy portraits. Named for the Fayum region where they were found in what was once Roman Egypt, more than one thousand mummy por-traits have been recovered. From the first through the third centuries, wealthy families often hired an artist to paint a loved one's portrait. The encaustic painting, a blend of dry pigment and soft wax, was done on a wooden tablet or linen cloth. After the person died, the portrait was placed on the face of the mummy for burial. The artists who painted these portraits gave their subjects haunting wide eyes and lifelike flesh tones.

Ancient Egyptian artists created this scene showing people harvesting crops.

Although most ancient Greek and Roman paintings were lost, written descriptions of many of them were passed down through the generations. Even unseen, these works of art would affect how life was recorded for centuries to come.

Tales of the Totem Pole

As early as 2,500 B.C., Native American cultures recorded history by painting images on bones, pottery, masks, and tepees. They also wove their stories and traditions into baskets, blankets, and rugs. Since the late 1700s, the Northwest coastal tribes of the United States and Canada have looked to the totem pole to keep their heritage alive. A wood totem pole is similar to a family crest. It is carved by skilled craftsworkers for a chief or the head of a clan, or family group. The figures on the pole trace family history and kinship, pay tribute to ancestors, and establish the status of its owner. The clan's totem, a spirit or animal guide, is also an important element. The ancient art of totem pole carving continues to thrive among the native people of the Pacific Northwest, British Columbia, and Alaska.

An Age of Wonder

In the middle of the fourteenth century, a new era was beginning in Europe. It was called the Renaissance. French for "rebirth," the Renaissance represented a revival of the arts and sciences first developed by the ancient Greeks and Romans. For the next two centuries, European artists, writers, scholars, and scientists would set their sights on discovering more about how the world worked. It was in this energetic atmosphere that inventions such as the printing press, microscope, and compass would be developed.

During the Renaissance, artists were no longer treated as manual laborers. Instead, they were viewed as highly skilled, important members of society. An artist was not merely a painter, but an explorer. A painting was not only a canvas, but a view to the world. Painters and sculptors studied nature in detail so they could precisely capture it in their work. In 1420, the new medium of oil painting provided artists with rich, dark colors to use. Renaissance art was realistic, bold, and full of emotion.

Florence, Italy, was the birthplace of the Renaissance. For a talented young artist and inventor named Leonardo da Vinci (1452–1519), there was no better place to call home. He kept detailed notebooks of his art and experiments. In 1490, da Vinci described in his journal an intriguing optical device he had seen: "When the images of illuminated objects pass through a small round hole into a very dark room, if you receive them on a piece of white paper placed vertically in the dark room at some distance from the *aperture,* you will see on the paper all those objects in their natural shapes and colours. They will be reduced in size, and upside down, owing to the intersection of the rays at the aperture."

Da Vinci was referring to what would become known as a *camera obscura.* Coined by German astronomer Johannes Kepler (1571–1630) in the seventeenth century, the term is Latin for "dark room." Here is how it worked. A beam of sunlight shining through a small hole in one wall of a darkened room would reflect an upside-down and reversed image of the scene outside onto the opposite wall. The views projected by the camera obscura were not an artist's conception of the world. They were the world. For the first time in history, people could see an image of life as it truly existed. This fascinated, and occasionally frightened, those who saw it.

This large camera obscura was mounted on two horizontal poles so it could be carried from place to place. The artist entered through a trap door in the floor to view the upside-down image on the back of a see-through screen.

"If you cannot paint, you can by this arrangement draw [the outline of the images] with a pencil. You will have then only to lay on the colours," explained Italian artist Giovanni Battista della Porta. He was one of the first to recognize the camera obscura's potential as a tracing and sketching tool. In time, inventors would make the camera obscura smaller and easier to use. Portable, shoebox-sized versions that could be tucked under the arm became popular among artists. In the mid-sixteenth century, a *lens* replaced the pinhole. Also, a mirror was placed inside the box to flip the reflection so it could be viewed right side up.

Early Spy Cams?

By the early eighteenth century, the camera obscura came in all shapes and sizes, from tents to table models to miniature inserts for walking sticks. One clever inventor designed a drinking goblet camera obscura. A tiny lens and mirror in the stem of the goblet projected an image onto the white wine inside the glass. A party host could use the device to spy on guests. Similarly, German schoolteacher Johann Christoph Kohlhans disguised his camera obscura as a book.

A Developing Dilemma

With its ability to reflect any scene from daily life, the camera obscura soon captivated the world. Yet the images it projected faded with the sunset. They were not permanent. Throughout the seventeenth and eighteenth centuries, a number of scientists would try to record the camera obscura's views. One of them was English chemist Thomas Wedgwood.

In 1725, German science professor Johann Heinrich Schulze accidentally discovered that silver nitrate—a mixture of nitric acid, chalk, and silver—darkened when exposed to the sun. In the late 1790s, Wedgwood expanded on this by using the same chemicals to copy images. In his experiments, he coated white leather (and sometimes paper) with silver nitrate. He then placed a painting that was done on glass over the leather, and he exposed both layers to sunlight. Within a few minutes, the leather turned black in the areas where the sun had hit it directly. It remained white in the places where sunlight had not been able to pass through the dark pigment of the painting. Wedgwood had created the world's first negative image. However, there were two big problems.

First, Wedgwood could not fix his images, or get them to remain. Even when taken out of the sun, the pictures continued getting darker until they were completely black. Second, he could not reproduce an image from the camera obscura. The reflections were simply too faint to make an impression on the silver nitrate. Wedgwood died in 1806, at the age of thirty-four, without finding a solution to these issues. But another person had been wondering if it was possible to make the camera obscura's images stay after the sun had set. Where others had failed, he would succeed.

CHAPTER THREE

FIRST PHOTOGRAPHER

The man who would take the world's first photograph was born on March 7, 1765, in Chalon-sur-Saône in east-central France. The third of four children, Joseph Niépce (pronounced Neeps) grew up in a loving, upper-class home. His mother, Anne-Claude, was from a well-known family. His father, Claude, held a high-ranking job collecting taxes for the king. Joseph was a shy, bright child. He

Inventor Joseph Niépce was born in 1765 and died in 1833.

19

was closest to his brother, Claude, who was two years older. The boys spent many hours together building miniature working models of machines.

Joseph intended to become a Catholic priest and was educated at the Pères de l'Oratoire religious school. He was a good student and excelled in physics, chemistry, and literature. In 1785, when he was just twenty years old,

The storming of the Bastille on July 14, 1789, signaled the beginning of the French Revolution.

his father died. Three years later, Joseph left school to join the national guard. Around that time, he took the name Nicéphore (pronounced Nee-say-fore). He would often sign his letters Joseph-Nicéphore, though most people came to call him Nicéphore.

In 1789, revolution broke out in France. Overwhelmed by soaring taxes, prices on goods, and unemployment, the poor rose up against those they believed were to blame: the upper classes and King Louis XVI. Being from a wealthy family that supported the king, Nicéphore knew his life would have been at risk. Reportedly, he fled the country during the early years of the French Revolution. He returned, however, in 1792 to enlist in the French army. His brother, Claude, also joined the military. In their letters, the brothers began to discuss how amazing it would be to fix the images produced by the camera obscura. But it would be more than twenty years before Nicéphore would focus seriously on the task.

Perseverance, Patience, and a Little Luck

By 1813, Nicéphore Niépce was a husband, father, and inventor. After leaving the French army in 1794, Nicéphore and Claude became business partners. They designed and received a *patent* for their invention of the *pyréolophore* (pye-ray-oh-loh-fore), the first internal combustion engine. Powered by coal and resin, the engine was intended to propel boats. Early experiments were successful, and the brothers believed their engine had great promise.

Transportation Innovation

In 1817, Claude and Nicéphore replaced the original coal and resin fuel in the pyréolophore with white oil of petroleum, a fuel similar to kerosene. "As a matter of fact if you succeed in injecting white oil of petroleum with enough energy to get instant vaporisation, it is sure, my dear friend, that you should obtain the most satisfying result," Nicéphore wrote to his brother. He was referring to a new way they had devised of delivering fuel to the engine. The pair would never know how important this discovery would be to the future of transportation. Today, nearly all gas- and diesel-powered automobiles run on the fuel-injection principle developed by the Niépce brothers.

While perfecting the pyréolophore, Nicéphore was drawn to a new art form called lithography. In this printing technique, an artist used a greasy crayon to draw on a stone plate. The plate was moistened with water and an oily ink applied with a roller. Because oil repels water, the ink would stick only to the lines drawn with the crayon. A print of the drawing could then be made by pressing paper against the plate. Nicéphore could not draw well, so his eighteen-year-old son, Isidore, made the designs. Nicéphore handled the printing. In his attic workroom, a curious Nicéphore went further. He placed transparent engravings on plates coated with his own type of light-sensitive varnish and exposed them to the sun. The inventor did not have much success making prints. But these projects did rekindle his interest in fixing images from the camera obscura.

In 1814, Isidore was drafted into the army. His father forged ahead alone. By 1816, Nicéphore was experimenting with silver compounds to produce a solvent that would make paper sensitive enough to pick up the faint reflec-

Nicéphore experimented with lithography, an art form that can be used to create portraits such as this one from the 1800s.

Nicephore's camera obscura is on display in a museum in France.

tions of the camera obscura. He also tinkered with the camera obscura itself, trying to construct one that would project stronger images.

During this time, Nicéphore experienced many setbacks. "You know from my last letter that I broke the lens of my camera obscura; but I had another which I was hoping to be able to put to good use," he wrote to Claude, who had traveled to Paris to promote the pyréolophore. "It was a false hope: the focus of this glass was shorter than the diameter of the box; so I could not use it."

Nicéphore did manage to craft a new camera obscura using the lens from his grandfather's old microscope and a ring box belonging to Isidore. Placing the device in a window, Nicéphore was able to get an image of a nearby birdhouse to appear on paper coated with silver chloride. But the picture was negative. Nicéphore had wanted to make a positive image, an exact duplicate of nature. Also, the image was not fixed and soon turned black. "I shall busy myself with three things," he wrote his brother. "First, to give more sharpness to the representation of the objects; second, to transpose the colours; third, finally, to fix them, which will not be the easiest. But as I have often told you, my dear friend, we have lots of patience and with patience one arrives at the end of all things."

Over the next four years, Nicéphore tried various chemicals, resins, and oils on different types of paper, stone, glass, and metal to create a positive print. Yet nothing gave him the results he was looking for. Finally, in the early 1820s, Nicéphore hit upon bitumen, a type of asphalt used by engravers. When exposed to the sun, bitumen not only lightened but also hardened. He found that when an engraving was placed on a bitumen-coated glass or metal plate, the areas exposed to sunlight would turn hard. Dissolving the hardened bitumen revealed a light gray, permanent, positive copy of the engraving on the plate. At last, he had done it! Now it was time to see if it was possible to record images of the real world.

In the summer of 1826, Nicéphore was ready. He had bought his first professionally made camera obscura and lens in Paris, and now he set it to face out of an upstairs window of his home. He placed a pewter plate coated with bitumen inside and took off the lens cap. After about eight hours of *exposure,* he removed the plate. He dissolved the hard bitumen with oil of lavender, turpentine, and lukewarm water. The result was a weak, but positive, image of part of his house, the barn roof, and the courtyard outside. The image was permanent. Success!

At age sixty-one, Nicéphore Niépce had taken the world's first photograph of nature. He referred to "View from the Window at Le Gras" as a *heliograph,* which means "sun

"View from the Window at Le Gras" was Nicéphore's first successful photograph.

writing" in Greek. Finally, the camera obscura could provide the world with permanent images. But for Nicéphore this victory would be short-lived.

A Genius Fades Away

In the fall of 1827, Nicéphore learned that Claude was sick. Nicéphore rushed to be with his brother, who was now living in England. Claude had moved there in 1817 to stir up interest in the pyréolophore. Despite devoting most of their lives and family fortune to the engine, the Niépce brothers had failed to find a market for it.

While in England, Nicéphore showed his heliographs to botanist Francis Bauer, a member of the Royal Society of London. The Royal Society was a panel of scientists who recognized major contributions to science. Bauer immediately realized the importance of Nicéphore's discovery and encouraged him to make a written presentation to the society.

On December 8, 1827, Nicéphore submitted an essay about his work, along with several heliographs. But in the report, he did not reveal the details of how he had achieved his results. Because of this, the society refused to give him credit for his research. It was a devastating blow. In January 1828, Nicéphore returned home. Before he left, he gave Bauer several of his heliographs, including "View from the Window at Le Gras." Claude died two weeks later.

A Treasure Lost . . . and Found

After an 1898 exhibition at the Crystal Palace in London, Niépce's "View from the Window at Le Gras" vanished. It would remain missing for more than fifty years. Its disappearance raised doubts as to just who had snapped the world's first photograph. In 1952, photo historians Helmut and Alison Gernsheim tracked down the heliograph. It had been locked in a trunk at a London storage facility.

In 1964, the Gernsheims donated the image to the Harry Ransom Humanities Research Center at the University of Texas in Austin. Now sealed in an airtight frame, the 8-by-6.5-inch (20-by-16.5-cm) plate is on exhibit at the center. On the back of the heliograph, Francis Bauer recorded the year, 1827, when Niépce gave him the print, along with these words: "Monsieur Niépce's first successful experiment of fixing permanently the Image from Nature." "View from the Window at Le Gras" proved, once and for all, who had taken the first photograph of nature. More than a century after his death, Nicéphore Niépce would receive the recognition he had never been given during his lifetime.

Deeply in debt, Nicéphore sold some of his family's property to survive. He went back to his attic, experimenting with silver plates and fumes of iodine to make better heliographs. In 1829, he was persuaded by French theater owner Louis Jacques Mandé Daguerre (pronounced duh-gair) to form a partnership for the purpose of improving camera obscura images. For years, Daguerre had also been trying to fix images from the device. On July 5, 1833, Nicéphore suffered a stroke at home and died. At the time, he was on the verge of bankruptcy. His achievements in photography had not been officially acknowledged.

Two years after Nicéphore's death, Daguerre found that silver iodide was more sensitive to light than bitumen. He successfully made a positive image on a silvered copper plate sensitized with iodine fumes. After exposure to sunlight for twenty minutes, the plate was held over a dish of heated mercury to bring out, or develop, the image. Further, Daguerre discovered he could fix the picture by washing the plate in a solution of warm water and table salt.

On August 19, 1839, Daguerre presented his process to the French Academy of Sciences. He called the image a *daguerreotype* (duh-gair-oh-type). It was an instant hit. Daguerre was given a lifetime pension, or regular payments, from France. He received numerous honors and worldwide licensing rights to the daguerreotype. Due to his father's agreement with Daguerre, Isidore Niépce was also awarded a lifetime pension. It was, however, a smaller sum, which angered Isidore, who believed Daguerre had profited unfairly from Nicéphore's years of research.

During his lifetime, Joseph-Nicéphore Niépce would receive no fame, glory, or fortune for his pioneering work in

This daguerreotype portrait of a man and young boy was taken by Daguerre sometime between 1847 and 1860.

photography. Yet history would not forget this man of vision and determination. He believed it was possible to capture a moment in time and was the first to make it happen.

CHAPTER FOUR

BEHIND THE LENS

In September 1839, optician shops throughout Paris were bustling with activity. Scientists and scholars were rushing to buy cameras, lenses, plates, and chemicals. Daguerre had teamed with French artist Alphonse Giroux to produce the first camera for sale to the public. "Daguerreotypomania," as the French newspapers called it, was rampant.

Many people, including American inventor Samuel Morse, had seen a demonstration of the daguerreotype. (Morse would take the technology back to America, where it would be met with even more excitement than in Europe.) The few who could afford the fifty dollar price, a large amount of money at the time, were buying their own cameras. Others bought a copy of

Daguerre's best-selling manual. The booklet provided step-by-step instructions on how to build a camera and make daguerreotypes.

The first daguerreotype camera was a bit smaller than today's standard microwave oven and weighed a little more than 12 pounds (5 kilograms). It consisted of two mahogany boxes—a smaller box that slid into a larger one. The bigger box housed a brass lens with an attached pivoting lens cap. The smaller one contained a mirror that flipped the image right side up and projected it onto a glass screen. The photographer focused the camera by sliding the rear box forward or back. When the shot was set, the photographer slipped the brass cap over the lens. The glass screen was removed from the back of the camera and replaced with a plate holder. The photographer slid a copper plate coated with silver iodide into the holder. There was no shutter. The exposure began the moment the lens cap was pushed away from the lens. At first, daguerreotype exposures took from three to fifteen minutes. But with improvements made over the course of about a year, the time of exposure was reduced to less than one minute.

The Ever-Changing Camera

As enthusiasm for the camera grew in Europe and America, inventors began improving its design. In August 1861, British photographer Thomas Sutton patented the single-lens reflex, or SLR, camera. Sutton's camera was a big, heavy box that used the same lens for viewing the scene as for taking the picture. A photographer held the camera waist high and peered down into it to see with near certainty the image that would be recorded on a plate.

An enduring design, the SLR is one of the most popular types of cameras among photographers today. Like its predecessor, the modern SLR lets the photographer view directly what the lens is seeing. A mirror and viewing prism, however, allow the camera to be held comfortably at eye level. Most SLRs now come equipped with electronic controls. A photographer may choose to set focus, *shutter* speed, and aperture manually or let the camera do it automatically.

Thomas Sutton also invented a panoramic camera that used a wide-angle lens with curved glass plates. These are the only surviving negatives produced by that camera.

The Camera

A camera is a lightproof box with a hole at one end and a light-sensitive material, such as a chemically coated plate, strip of film, or an electronic sensor at the other. The image passes through the lens to an aperture, an opening that is controlled by the iris diaphragm. The diaphragm is made of thin, overlapping metal blades that slide open from the center. It allows a photographer to regulate the amount of light that reaches the light-sensitive material. The diaphragm is described by its f-number, or *f-stop*. The shutter, a feature that was added in the 1870s, gives a photographer control over how long the image is exposed. It is located between the aperture and the light-sensitive material. The shutter is a small spring-activated plate or disc. (On a digital camera, the shutter is electronic.) On exposure, it quickly slides away to allow a split second of light into the camera, then quickly moves back into place. Shutter speed is expressed in fractions: 1/15 means an exposure of one-fifteenth of a second, 1/60 is one-sixtieth of a second, and so on. The f-stop and shutter work together to regulate the amount of light that reaches the light-sensitive material so that proper exposure can be achieved.

By the late nineteenth century, cameras were becoming smaller and lighter. The 1880s became the decade of the detective camera. A person could "play detective" and snap photos unnoticed. Originally, these cameras were disguised as books to allow the police to watch suspected criminals. But they quickly captured the eye of the public, and other

The interior of an SLR camera

designs soon followed. Detective cameras masqueraded as handbags, binoculars, watches, and articles of clothing. Most detective cameras had tiny, cheap lenses, and the pictures did not come out well. Even so, the craze did bring to light a new aspect of photography: People could be photographed without their knowledge or consent.

Fatal Flashes

Photographers first began to use flash powder in the 1860s. When heated, the explosive mixture of magnesium and other chemicals created a brief burst of light. Flash powder gave photographers the freedom to shoot pictures anywhere and at any time, even at night. Unfortunately, the unpredictable nature of the explosive mixture cost many photographers their fingers, hands, and, sometimes, their lives. In 1925, Austrian inventor Paul Vierkötter enclosed magnesium foil in a vacuum inside a glass bulb, creating the flashbulb. A battery sent an electrical current through the wire to set off the charge. Although safer than powder, flashbulbs were not risk free. They could explode unexpectedly, raining bits of glass on those standing nearby. Today, nearly all cameras rely on electronic flashes powered by batteries.

Shutterbug Fever

In barely a half century, the camera had come a long way from its bulky beginnings. Still, photography was not something the average person was likely to try. Quality camera gear was expensive. Glass plates were awkward and fragile. To process photos, people had to construct their own darkrooms and use dangerous chemicals.

American inventor George Eastman believed that more people would take up photography if the equipment were simpler to use. In the early 1880s, he founded a photography supply company in Rochester, New York. The inventor set to work to make "the camera as convenient as the pencil." In 1888, Eastman introduced the Kodak camera (always partial to the letter K, Eastman made up the word *Kodak* himself). The handheld camera had a fixed lens, one shutter speed, and a set f-stop. There was no viewfinder, or window through the body of the camera, so photographers had to "point and shoot," hoping they had framed the shot correctly. (In contrast, most of today's fully automatic point-and-shoot models contain a viewfinder.)

Eastman also thought up an advertising catchphrase: "You press the button, we do the rest." It was no exaggeration. Each Kodak camera came preloaded with enough film for one hundred pictures. Once all of the exposures had been taken, the camera was simply mailed back to the company, along with $10. At the plant, the film was developed, round 2.5-inch (6-cm) prints were made, and a new roll of film was inserted into the camera. The prints and camera were then mailed back to their owner.

By the end of the first year, Eastman had sold 5,000 cameras and was processing seventy rolls of film a day. But at $25, the Kodak was too expensive. The average worker earned only $32 a month. Eastman went back to the drawing board to make a more affordable device. In 1900, he unveiled the Brownie. Named after a popular cartoon character, the camera cost just $1; a roll of film was 15 cents. The Brownie was marketed to children

Eastman invented the Brownie camera in 1900.

but caught the attention of adults, too. Kodak sold 150,000 Brownies its first year, and millions more as the series continued for the next seventy years.

As the twentieth century dawned, photography was no longer limited to the experts or the well-to-do. George Eastman had turned a complicated technique into a relaxing hobby. Everyone capable of pointing a camera and pressing a button could experience the "magic" of photography for themselves.

A Photo Finish: Processing and Printing

As the first true form of photography, the daguerreotype enjoyed immense popularity. But it had one fatal flaw: it could not be duplicated. Each copper plate was a one-of-a kind creation. The challenge of making multiple prints would fall to an Englishman named William Henry Fox Talbot.

During the mid-1830s Talbot was experimenting with light-sensitive paper. In 1839, he read an article about Daguerre's research. He worried the daguerreotype sounded a lot like his own unpatented photogenic drawings. Talbot would soon discover that he had nothing to fear. The two techniques were quite different.

To make a photogenic drawing, Talbot bathed paper in a salt solution, then coated it with silver nitrate. He placed it in a camera obscura and obtained a negative in less than three minutes. The image was developed by brushing on more silver nitrate, then fixed with a potassium iodide solution. By placing another piece of sensitized paper over the negative and exposing both layers to sunlight for ten minutes, Talbot was able to create a positive print from the negative. Even better, he could make an unlimited number of positive copies from the original negative.

Talbot created photographs that he called calotypes using these cameras.

Talbot's process of making multiple positive prints from a single negative was a huge breakthrough in processing. It established the framework for how photographs are developed today. Talbot patented his process in 1841. He renamed his photogenic drawings *calotypes,* Greek for "beautiful impressions." Talbot would go on to write *The Pencil of Nature*, a six-volume book about the calotype. Published between 1844 and 1847, it was the first printed book to use photographs in its pages.

As demand for the camera grew, advancements in processing and printing came quickly. In ten years, both the daguerreotype and calotype would be replaced by the wet collodion, or wet plate, process. Invented by English

This peaceful scene was captured using the wet collodion process.

engraver Frederick Scott Archer (1813–1857) in 1850, glass plates were coated with collodion. This clear, thick liquid was produced by soaking cotton in nitric and sulfuric acids, then dissolving it in alcohol and ether. From the negative, positive images were often printed on albumen paper, which was paper coated with a mixture of egg whites, potassium iodide, and iodine.

By the end of the 1850s, tintypes, positive collodion prints made directly onto thin sheets of darkened iron or steel, were easy to make and inexpensive. During the American Civil War (1861–1865), millions of soldiers purchased tintype portraits of themselves to send to friends and families back home. The wet collodion process shortened exposure times to about three seconds. Even so, it was a messy and inconvenient way to shoot photos. A photographer was required to coat the plate with chemicals immediately prior to taking the picture. After exposure, the image had to be developed and fixed before the

These African American soldiers were just two of the many soldiers who had tintype portraits of themselves taken during the Civil War.

plate had time to dry. This meant photographers had to haul around chemicals, equipment, and a portable tent or wagon to serve as a darkroom.

Within about fifteen years, dry plates precoated with an *emulsion* of silver bromide and gelatin became available in Europe. Dry plates did not have to be exposed and developed right away. But they were also much less sensitive to light than collodion. This lengthened exposure times.

In the early 1880s, George Eastman set out to find a lighter, more flexible material to replace the glass plates. After numerous experiments, Eastman hit upon the answer: a strip of paper coated with collodion and treated with a gelatin emulsion. In 1884, he hired camera designer William H. Walker. Together, the two devised a wooden frame to hold the roll of paper film. Their frame could fit on the back of almost any plate camera. Now, instead of sliding a glass plate into a holder for every new picture, a photographer had only to turn a key to advance the roll of film.

Eastman and Walker had made picture taking easier. Eastman wanted buyers of the camera to understand how easy it was to use. So he rewrote the complicated instruction manual that had been created by a professional writer. Eastman's version of the directions read in part:

1—Pull the String
2—Turn the Key
3—Press the Button

A Sure Bet

In 1872, railroad tycoon and former governor of California Leland Stanford bet a friend $25,000 that when a horse gallops, there is a moment when all four hooves are off the ground at the same time. Stanford hired photographer Eadweard Muybridge to prove his theory. It took Muybridge six years to devise the equipment needed to accomplish the task. On June 15, 1878, he set up twelve electrically controlled, high-speed cameras around the racetrack at Stanford's ranch in Palo Alto, California. Each shutter was rigged with a wire that stretched across the width of the track. As Stanford's horse, Abe Edgington, trotted past each camera, the wheels of the horse's carriage rolled over the wires and released the shutters. The sequence of photos not only helped Stanford win his bet but led to the development of motion pictures.

Paper film worked well enough, except the grain of the paper kept showing through on the images. In 1889, one of Eastman's chemists, Henry Reichenbach, solved the problem. He devised a transparent film that used a nitrocellulose backing instead of paper. The strong transparent film paved the way for early motion picture cameras, such as Thomas Edison's kinetoscope (1894) and Louis and Auguste Lumière's cinématographe (1895). Nitrocellulose film would be used by photographers and filmmakers for more than forty years, until it was replaced by less-flammable plastics such as acetate and polyester. In 1935, Kodak would take the photography world by storm once again with the introduction of color roll film.

In less than a century, people had not only invented photography but dramatically altered its equipment and processing methods. Lighter cameras, better lenses, faster film—inventors kept pushing the limits to see how far the technology would go. Of course, while humans were focused on changing the face of photography, they would discover that photography, in turn, was also changing the world.

CHAPTER FIVE

THE UNBLINKING EYE

Julia Margaret Cameron took this photograph in 1866.

Legend has it that when French artist Paul Delaroche (1797–1856) saw the daguerreotype, he declared, "From today, painting is dead." Whether or not Delaroche actually said this, it was certainly true that the advent of photography was shaking up the art world.

People were flocking to have their pictures taken by what American physician, author, and photogra-

47

phy buff Oliver Wendell Holmes dubbed "the mirror with a memory." To earn a living, many portrait painters in Europe and America traded in their brushes for cameras. In 1853, there were more than one hundred portrait photography studios in the United States. At first, a photo portrait cost about $15. But it wasn't long before competition drove the price down to just a few dollars, making portraits within the reach of most everyone.

Carte-de-visite

French photographer André Adolphe Disdéri started a craze for carte-de-visite (cart duh vee-zeet), a miniature portrait mounted on a trading card. It became fashionable for people to put their photograph on the 2.5-by-4-inch (6-by-10-cm) cards and swap them with friends and relatives. Most every family kept their collection of tiny portraits in a photo album. People could also buy cartes-de-visite of famous people, such as Queen Victoria or Abraham Lincoln.

Initially, photographers were not considered true artists. Many critics claimed photographs were not art because they were produced by a machine, the way fabric was made from a loom. Yet others, particularly Americans, agreed with Samuel Morse that photography would "bring about a new standard in art." Indeed, many

Actress Sarah Bernhardt posed for these cartes-de-visite in the 1860s.

traditional artists found photography gave them a new way to express themselves. Through lighting, focus, composition, and processing, a photographer could create a masterpiece on a plate the way a painter did on canvas. England's Julia Margaret Cameron (1815–1879) shot her subjects slightly out of focus, producing artistic pictures with soft outlines and angelic-looking expressions.

In the latter half of the nineteenth century, photographers worked hard to gain artistic acceptance. They held exhibitions, established clubs, and published professional journals. Eventually, the art world began to understand that just as a typewriter could not write a novel, neither could a camera take a picture. Only the keen and talented eye of a human being could create extraordinary images. In time, people would come to see that photography could breathe new life into the art of creating images—a craft that was as old as humanity itself.

A Window to the World

In the days before airplanes made traveling around the globe common, most people rarely journeyed more than a few miles from home. Knowledge of distant lands, faraway cultures, and current events was limited. The camera, however, would help to change all that. Before newspapers were capable of printing photographs, many people got their first glimpse of the world beyond their backyard through a *stereoscope.* The binocular viewer was invented in 1849 by Scottish physicist David Brewster, who also devised the kaleidoscope. It was meant for looking at special photo cards, called *stereographs.* On each card, two images of the same scene taken at slightly different angles were mounted side by side. When seen through a stereoscope, the photos appeared as a single three-dimensional picture.

In the middle of the nineteenth century, stereographs were as popular in the United States as television is today. Families would gather in the evening to pass around the handheld viewer to look at an assortment of cards. They would glimpse lush landscapes, great works of art, and foreign societies half a world away. Important news stories, including the Chicago fire of 1871 and the San Francisco earthquake of 1906, also found their way onto stereographs.

Viewing special photo cards called stereographs through a stereoscope was a popular family entertainment in the late 1800s.

A woman views stereographs in her home.

Little by little, the camera was expanding human understanding of Earth. It was opening people's eyes. Of course, the trouble with opening your eyes is that, sometimes, you might not like what you see.

The Power of Pictures

"A spirit in my feet said 'go,' and I went," explained Mathew Brady on why he left his successful New York portrait studio to lead a team of photographers onto the battlefields of the American Civil War. In the early 1860s, Brady, Alexander Gardner, Timothy O'Sullivan, Thomas C. Roche, and other pioneers of *photojournalism* documented the aftermath of many battles. On the home front, Americans were moved by the graphic images. "Mr. Brady

Photographer Mathew Brady was born in 1823 and died in 1896. He was a pioneer in the field of photojournalism.

has done something to bring home to us the terrible reality and earnestness of war," reported *The New York Times.*

"Here are the dreadful details!" Gardner wrote regarding his photos of dead soldiers. "Let them aid in preventing another such calamity falling upon the nation."

Photographs were proving to be a powerful force for change—sometimes even more powerful than words. Startling

Lewis Hine's photographs of dirty, exhausted children covered in coal dust helped bring about the passage of laws to protect children who worked in mines and factories.

images could open the eyes of a society that could not, or would not, see its own challenges. In the late 1880s, Danish immigrant Jacob Riis's photos of overcrowded and filthy apartment buildings in New York prompted the city to improve housing for the poor. Similarly, the images taken by Lewis Hine of exhausted child laborers covered in coal dust spoke louder than any statistics published by the National Child Labor Committee. Such photos pressured many states to enact laws against allowing children to work long hours in mills, mines, and factories. "There are two things that I wanted to do," said Hine. "I wanted to show the things that needed to be corrected. I wanted to show the things that needed to be appreciated."

A Haunting Face

In the 1930s, photographer Dorothea Lange lived out of her car for several months as she followed migrant farmworkers in the Dust Bowl during the Great Depression. One of Lange's most famous photographs, "Migrant Mother" (1936), portrayed a young woman who arrived at a California farm to pick peas only to learn that bad weather had ruined the crop. "I did not ask her name or her history," Lange would later recall. "She told me her age, that she was thirty-two. She said that they had been living on frozen vegetables from the surrounding fields, and birds that [her] children killed. She had just sold the tires from her car to buy food. There she sat in that lean-to tent with her children huddled around her, and seemed to know that my pictures might help her, and so she helped me." When Lange's photo ran in newspapers across the country, the public sent more than 22,000 pounds (10,000 kg) of food to the farm.

Then, as today, people peered through the viewfinder to bring injustice, tragedy, and heartache to light. And when these images touched people, they were inspired to make changes.

CHAPTER SIX

INSTANT IMAGES

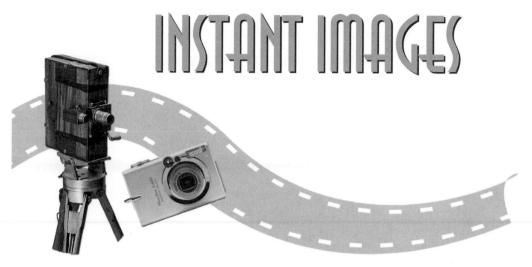

As the twentieth century unfolded, the camera was no longer a novelty. It was a necessity. It influenced virtually every aspect of modern life. It spread news, spawned entertainment, fueled politics, and set trends. What had begun as a simple box with a lens was now an important instrument for connecting and shaping humankind. Even as the camera was finding its place in society, however, the world was beginning to change.

New inventions such as the automobile, diesel engine, and airplane were revolutionizing transportation. Radio, motion pictures, and television were simplifying global communication. Life in the new century was changing rapidly. Innovative minds would be challenged to design cameras that could keep up.

A Revolution in Photography

In 1925, the Leitz Company of Germany, which specialized in making microscopes, introduced a new type of camera. Engineer Oskar Barnack had turned a device used for taking samples of cinematic film into a 35 millimeter, or 35mm, camera. The Leica, a blend of the words *Leitz* and *camera*, improved upon the Tourist Multiple and Simplex 35mm cameras, which were introduced in 1913. (The term *35mm camera* comes from using film that is 35 millimeters wide.) The Leica was small enough to fit into a coat pocket, yet it produced images far superior to anything that had come before it. Further, it allowed a photographer to change lenses in the middle of a roll of film, offered shutter speeds up to 1/500 of a second, and made it possible to take a series of pictures in rapid succession.

Many U.S. photojournalists preferred the Leica. Within ten years, the **Associated Press (AP)** would begin transmitting photos by telegraph wire to newspapers instead of sending them through the mail. AP wire photos, in combination with the 35mm camera, would introduce a new age in mass media. High-quality photos could be snapped in seconds and sent out within hours to appear in newspapers across the country the same day. Several magazines, such as *Look* and *Life*, were founded to take advantage of the explosion in photojournalism. Launched in 1936, *Life* made famous the pictorial essay, a collage of photos that told a story with minimal text.

With the addition of automatic focus, flash, and film advance, the 35mm format would remain at the forefront of photography through the twentieth century and beyond. At the beginning of the twenty-first century, Photo Marketing Association International reported that 35mm cameras were still the most popular type of camera purchased and used in the United States.

The 35mm Leica camera revolutionized photography when it was introduced to the public in 1925.

Noteworthy Twentieth-Century Cameras

Name, Country & Date of Origin	Description
1900 – The Mammoth *United States*	The camera was 20 feet (6 m) long and weighed 1400 pounds (620 kg), requiring a crew of 15 people to operate it.
1912 – Doppel-Sport *Denmark*	Devised to be strapped to a homing pigeon, the miniature camera featured a swiveling lens and time-release shutter.
1946 – Phantom *England*	An all-in-one unit with developing tanks and contact printer inside the camera, which also doubled as an enlarger and projector.
1948 – Sakura Petal *Japan*	About the size of a U.S. quarter and slightly thicker, the Petal is one of the smallest commercial cameras ever made.
1969 – Hasselblad EDC *Sweden*	A motorized electric data camera designed for NASA, it had special controls so astronauts could use it while wearing thick space gloves.

Photo Facts

The Mammoth took 8-by-4-foot (2-by-1-m) photos of trains for the Chicago & Alton Railroad.

As they soared over enemy territory, these "fly spies" snapped the earliest aerial reconnaissance photos.

In 2001, a Phantom sold at auction for more than $200,000, making it the most valuable camera in the world.

Originally retailing for $20 in the United States, today a Petal in good condition is valued at about $400.

Apollo XI astronauts used EDCs to snap the first photos of humans walking on the Moon's surface.

The Mammoth camera was created to take a picture of a Chicago & Alton Railroad train that was at least 8 (2.4 m) feet long.

See It Now

In 1929, twenty-year-old Edwin Land (1909–1991), an American physicist, patented Polaroid, a plastic sheet

Edwin Land founded the Polaroid Corporation in 1937.

of crystals that filtered sunlight. The substance became widely used on camera and microscope filters and sunglasses to reduce glare.

Fourteen years later, while on vacation, the gifted scientist snapped a photo of his three-year-old daughter, Jennifer. She asked why they could not see the picture right away. Intrigued by this question, Land set to work to design a camera that could produce photographs on the spot. By 1948, he created it. The Model 95 Polaroid Land camera held all the chemicals needed to process photos in a film pack inside the cam-

The Model 95 Polaroid Land camera became available to the public in 1948.

era. After exposure, the photographer grabbed a single tab, which pulled both the negative and positive paper through a pair of stainless steel rollers. This caused a capsule containing developing and fixing chemicals to burst open and coat the paper. In less than a minute, the black-and-white picture developed inside the camera. The photographer

Pictures developed inside the early Polaroid cameras. The photographer opened the back of the camera and peeled the print away from the negative.

had only to remove the image from the back of the camera and peel the positive print away from its negative.

In 1972, Polaroid made available the SX-70 point-and-shoot system. Two seconds after the shutter was released, the camera produced a photo that gradually developed right before the photographer's eyes. Polaroid cameras were an instant success; Americans rushed to buy them. Still, the race to create instant images was far from over.

Welcome to the Digital Age

In the 1960s, the National Aeronautics and Space Administration (NASA) launched unmanned space probes to photograph the moon's surface. But the images being transmitted back to Earth were fuzzy. Receivers on Earth had difficulty picking up the signals from so far away.

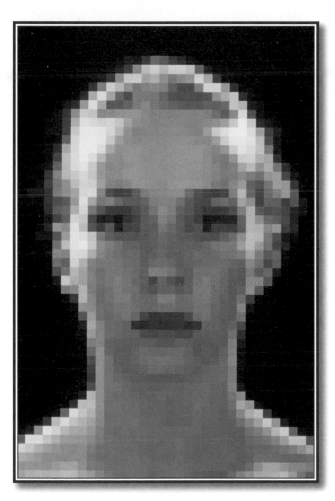

Digital photographs are made up of hundreds of thousands of pixels.

NASA engineers solved the problem by inventing digital computer processing. Images were sent back one picture element, or *pixel,* at a time. A pixel is a tiny square dot of color. (If you look very closely at a digital photograph, you'll see it is made up of hundreds of thousands, perhaps millions, of pixels.) When the camera onboard a spacecraft

Before saving a digital photograph, a photographer can use software to correct colors and make other changes to the image.

66

took a photo, each pixel was assigned a number. The number was then transmitted back to Earth to be read by a computer and recombined with other pixels to form the original image. At first, digital photos were black-and-white. The advent of red, green, and blue pixels allowed for the creation of full-color images.

In the early 1970s, researchers at Kodak began working to create a digital camera. They succeeded. In 1991, the Dycam Model 1 and Kodak DCS 100 became the first true digital cameras available to the public. Instead of using film, a digital camera relies on a light-sensitive electronic chip and a computer to record images electronically. Photos are stored on a removable *memory card.* A digital camera is usually characterized by how many millions of pixels it is capable of capturing. More pixels means a better quality, or higher resolution, image. For example, a five *megapixel* camera will produce sharper images than a three megapixel camera.

After a photo has been taken, a liquid crystal display, or LCD, monitor on the digital camera allows the image to be viewed right away. The image may be erased, downloaded onto a computer, or sent directly to a printer. Before storing the photo on computer or compact disk, the photographer may decide to manipulate it. Photographic software allows the elimination of red-eye, the addition or deletion of elements, the creation of special effects, and the correction of color, brightness, or contrast.

Faking Photos

Computer software has made it easier than ever to manipulate photos and harder to detect photos that have been altered. Yet the art of altering images is not new. In the days of the daguerreotype, artists would often paint a waterfall, castle, or garden background onto a portrait. The age of competitive photojournalism, however, prompted practices that were far less benign. Photographers who worked for William Randolph Hearst, owner of the largest chain of U.S. newspapers in the early twentieth century, admitted violating ethical standards by tampering with photos. Objects in photos were often cloned, removed, or combined with other photos to create sensational pictures that would increase newspaper sales. Today, most news organizations make it a policy not to alter photos, but many other publications, such as fashion magazines and tabloids, have no such standards.

Picture This!

When digital cameras were first introduced, many experts concluded they would be a passing fad. It quickly became clear, however, that digital technology was the wave of the future. In 2003, after only thirteen years on the market, sales of digital camera surpassed those of traditional film cameras. By 2004, close to 40 percent of all households in the United States owned at least one digital camera. Research groups predict about 70 percent of Americans will own a digital camera within the next few years as the technology improves and the prices drop.

Advancements in digital photography have also made it easier than ever to snap pictures anywhere, anytime. In 2000, Japan's Sharp Electronics introduced a cellular phone equipped with a digital camera. Within five years, 80 percent of all cellular phones in that country had cameras. The trend is now sweeping the globe. Hundreds of millions of camera phones are sold worldwide each year. In 2001, SMal Camera Technologies in Cambridge, Massachusetts, made its Ultra-Pocket camera available to the public. About the size of a credit card, it was the thinnest digital camera in the world. The Ultra-Pocket automatically adjusts light levels, so a flash isn't necessary. Also, the battery recharges itself each time the tiny camera is connected to a computer.

Where will the camera go from here? Its future lies in the hands of pioneering inventors who continue to find new ways to make the device more practical and efficient. Although the camera's design is constantly changing, its legacy remains the same: to portray the best and the worst; the familiar and the unknown; the past, the present, and the future.

THE CAMERA: A TIMELINE

Renaissance artists use the camera obscura as a tracing and sketching tool.
p. 16

Niépce takes the world's first photograph, "View from the Window at Le Gras."
p. 26

Daguerre reveals the daguerreotype to the world and markets the first camera.
pp. 29–31

Thomas Sutton patents the single-lens reflex camera.
pp. 32–33

1500s 1813 1826 1834–1835 1839 1841 1860s 1861

Nicéphore Niépce begins trying to fix images from the camera obscura.
p. 22

William Henry Fox Talbot begins experimenting with photogenic drawings.
p. 40

Talbot makes multiple images from a single negative.
p. 40

Photographers use flash powder to create artificial light.
p. 36

George Eastman invents a hand-held film camera, the Kodak.
p. 37

Kodak releases Kodachrome, color film for 35mm slides and movies.
pp. 45–46

The Leitz Company launches the 35mm camera; the flashbulb is invented.
p. 58

NASA devises digital imaging to enhance photographs transmitted from space.
pp. 65–66

The first cellular phone equipped with a camera becomes available to the public.
p. 69

1878	1888	1889	1925	1935	1948	1960s	1991	2000

Eadweard Muybridge photographs a horse in motion, laying the groundwork for motion pictures.
p. 45

Eastman's company makes transparent film, supplying Thomas Edison and others with rolls to use in motion pictures.
p. 45

Edwin Land pioneers the era of instant images with the Polaroid camera.
p. 63

The Dycam Model 1 and Kodak DCS 100, the first true digital cameras, are made available to the public.
p. 66

GLOSSARY

aperture: the opening of the lens of a camera, which allows light to enter

Associated Press (AP): a cooperative of U.S. newspapers that gathers and distributes news stories, photos, and broadcasts to its members around the world

calotypes: negative photographic images that allow for multiple positive images to be made from the same negative

camera obscura: a room or box with a small opening in which light reflects an inverted and reversed image of an outside scene on an opposite wall or piece of paper

daguerreotype: an early photographic process in which a positive image was produced, developed, and fixed on a silver-coated and sensitized copper plate

digital camera: a camera that records and stores images electronically

emulsion: a thin, light-sensitive coating of chemicals mixed with gelatin or other binding material that is applied to plates or film

exposure: the amount of light let into a camera

f-stop: an aperture setting for a lens that is determined by dividing the diameter of the aperture into the focal length of the lens

heliograph: a positive photographic image made on a sensitized metal plate

lens: one or more pieces of curved, polished glass that act as the eye of a camera

megapixel: one million pixels in a digital camera's electronic light sensor

memory card: a type of card or stick that is inserted into a digital camera to store photographic images

ochre: red or yellow iron ore that can be used to make pigment

Paleolithic: the early part of the Stone Age, from 750,000 to 15,000 years ago

patent: a document issued by a government agency giving the applicant exclusive rights to make or sell an invention

photojournalism: a form of journalism in which photos play a more important role in telling the story than the accompanying text

pixel: one of the many square dots of color that comprise a digital image; short for "picture element"

portrait: a drawing, painting, or photograph of a person

shutter: a device for regulating a camera's exposure time

stereograph: a card featuring two nearly identical photos mounted side by side; when viewed through a stereoscope, the photos appeared as a single three-dimensional image

stereoscope: a binocular viewer used to view a photo called a stereograph

TO FIND OUT MORE

Books

Czech, Kenneth P. *Snapshot: America Discovers the Camera.* Minneapolis: Lerner Publications, 1996.

Johnson, Neil. *National Geographic Photography Guide for Kids.* Washington, DC: National Geographic Society, 2001.

Partridge, Elizabeth. *Restless Spirit: The Life and Work of Dorothea Lange.* New York: Puffin Books, 2001.

Pflueger, Lynda. *George Eastman: Bringing Photography to the People.* Berkeley Heights, NJ: Enslow Publishers, 2002.

Varriale, Jim. *Take a Look Around: Photography Activities for Young People.* Brookfield, CT: Millbrook Press, 1999.

DVDs

Digital Photography: The Camera. Media West Home Video, 2003.

National Geographic: The Photographers. National Geographic, 2000.

Web Sites

Harry Ransom Humanities Research Center

www.hrc.utexas.edu/exhibitions/permanent/wfp

University of Texas at Austin

P.O. Box 7219

Austin, TX 78713-7219

See the first photograph, "View from the Window at Le Gras," and learn how historians are preserving it today.

Nicéphore Niépce House

www.niepce.com/home-us.html

8 Rue Jules Vallès

75011 Paris, France

Discover more about the first photographer and see some of his lesser-known inventions.

Organizations

George Eastman House

International Museum of Photography and Film

900 East Avenue

Rochester, NY 14607

www.eastmanhouse.org

Read more about the life and inventions of George Eastman.

INDEX

ABOUT THE AUTHOR

An award-winning photographer and broadcast journalist, Trudi Strain Trueit says her passion for photography began when she got her first camera in the fourth grade. Since then, she has spent plenty of time on both sides of the lens. She has worked as a news reporter and photographer for several newspaper and televisions stations throughout the Pacific Northwest.

Ms. Trueit has authored more than twenty books for Scholastic on nature, weather, health, and history. Some of her titles include *Clouds*, *Storm Chasers*, *Earthquakes*, and *Gunpowder*.

Born in Seattle, Ms. Trueit has a degree in broadcast journalism and lives in Everett, Washington. She loves to travel with her husband, Bill, who is also a photographer, capturing images whenever she can.